I0480551

Those in need of a priceless treasure with infinite power – HOPE. Let a billion hopes rise from the depths of darkness and light up the world.

I gratefully acknowledge all the help and those endless hours of deliberations with the SKILSertifika team who made this book possible – T.C. Dhoundiyal, Madhuri Chawhan, Divyanshu Choudhary, Toshali Sharma and Shivam Dabral.

I also gratefully acknowledge help of six more people; without whose help this book wouldn't have shaped up: - Dr. Debashis Sanyal (My PhD Supervisor), Jayanti Dasgupta (my wife), Juhi Rajput (my Sister, who has been a pillar of support for long), My Dad – Dr. S. K. Dasgupta, My Sister. Ranjini and Tapasya Datta (my ex-student, who constantly cheered me up).

Dr. S. Dasgupta
(First Author)

FOREWORD

Who should read this book?

We are facing a "Once-In-A-Century" challenge with the COVID-19 crisis and the third economic revolution. Our generation is simultaneously fortunate and unfortunate to face this challenge. But being fortunate or unfortunate is IN YOUR HANDS! This is the key message of the book. It's up to you to build RESILIENCE and face this challenge. This challenge represents the Valley of Death. In a valley of death, you can only go forward, you can never go backward and restore back to your old status!

Hence you have two choices:- a) either try to restore back your past – you may remain an unfortunate victim and fade away b) understand that LIFE WILL NEVER BE THE SAME again and you will emerge from the Valley of Death a different person: - stronger and better and lead a new life. So being fortunate is in your own hands.

This book first explains what this "once-in-a-century" challenge is all about in chapter 2. Next through a series of twelve gripping adventure stories the book demonstrates how resilience can be built. In the final chapter the book briefly demonstrates how to innovate in face of crisis and emerge stronger with twelve principles of COUNTER INTUITIVE thinking, resembling King Arthur's Twelve Knights of his round table.

So! Resilience is your EXCALIBUR – King Arthur's legendary sword of justice! This book can be read by the young and the old, from any back-

*ground who are facing a serious challenge of survival and draw inspir-
ation & hope, build resilience and PUSH FORWARD IN ANY SPHERE OF
LIFE.*

Note: *If you are short of patience and time, then please read only the
last chapter to understand the twelve key lessons and apply them in
your own life, both in personal and professional spheres. This Chapter
is the USP & key takeaway of the Book. This book is part of a two- part
series named: INNOVATION IN VALLEY OF DEATH.*

*The second book delves deeper into the topic of innovation, grounded
in academic theory of Dynamic Capabilities, replete with real life case
studies to demonstrate how to innovate in crisis situations and mainly
addresses a managerial and entrepreneurial audience. While the first
book is for all – can be read and lessons applied by anyone in any sphere
of life.*

THE SKILLSERTIFIKA TEAM

TABLE OF CONTENT

CHAPTER 1

Introduction

The Current Covid-19 Crisis has taken the world by storm and turned it upside down. But we have to see beyond and behind the crisis. Pandemics have appeared from time to time in history of the world, like the Spanish plague in 1918, which resulted in more than a million deaths. But aftermath the Spanish plague came the mass produced automobile, wireless and the aircraft and these three innovations changed the 20th century civilisation, giving rise to Multinational companies operating across the globe with a multi- divisional structure and innovations like management accounting, brand management, formalized strategic planning, matrix organizations, foreign currency trading and convertibility of currency, international laws, WTO and the World Bank-IMF shaped the global economy as we know it today along with the fortune 500 giants.

So! The historical perspective of economic revolutions is often missed and overlooked in a maze of economic modelling and data crunching. As Winston Churchill once remarked: - *"The deeper you look into the past the further you can foresee the future"*. Two economic revolutions occurred in global business history and the third one – WE ARE RIGHT IN MIDDLE OF IT. The first one was steam based and occurred in 19th century, was powered by the steam engine, railways, telegraph and steamship – which gave rise to the first wave of Globalization between 1870 and 1913. This wave ended with WW 1 and was followed by the Spanish plague pandemic. Post pandemic the oil-based revolution picked up, powered by the mass-produced automobile and Henry Ford's MODEL-T. This revolution triggered a second round of Globalization, which commenced in 1930s post-depression and was briefly halted during the WW 2 years. Post WW 2 this wave picked up and gathered momentum in 1950s. By early 1990s this wave resulted in all modern management and technology innovations we have witnessed and most of us have grown up with.

The third revolution probably commenced with advent of internet, Windows operating system and laying down of transatlantic communication cables in mid 1990s. today after 25 years this revolution has gathered momentum and Post Covid-19, the world will look completely different.

Here let us briefly explain, what are the elements of an ECONOMIC REVOLUTION?

It normally commences with Technology, then pervades social structures, leading to changing consumer behaviour and finally gives rise to new kinds of business forms, companies. So, there are three elements: -

a) Technology – the digital and exponential technologies of today

b) Changing consumer behaviour and social structures – for example today's young generation is shunning all 20th century middle class values – "educate yourself – take up a steady job – get married – take housing and car loans – raise a family – retire from the company you joined". They neither want to be in a full-time job, nor want to identify themselves with any company for life long. They are not interested in burdening themselves with loans and nor want to buy a car or a house with loans. This has affected two sectors badly – automobiles -the small car market has virtually evaporated, due to car sharing practices, radio cabs companies like UBER, efficient public transport systems like the metro and rising aspirations and banking.

c) Energy revolution – from steam to oil to renewable energies. Many of us have grown up with power cuts. For the first time in history of mankind the promise of abundant and cheap energy (almost at a negligible cost) is about to become a reality and the energy revolution will give rise to SMART power grids and cities.

So, there is a VERY BIG DISRUPTION HAPPENING OUT THERE, it is just not disruption of technology as pointed out by the Late Clayton Christensen in 1997, in his book: - "The Innovator's dilemma". Professor Chris talked about disruptive technology giving rise to newer industries and destroying older ones.

Today what is happening is just not disruption of technology BUT DISRUPTION OF ECONOMICS.

Just like 1918, the third economic revolution combined with COVID-19 is changing everything around us and all that we know, all that we learnt is up in the air, causing loss of hope, depression, joblessness, and panic all around. New frameworks, new thoughts, new approaches, new business models and new organization structures will spring up post COVID. The Government of India is attempting to usher in some fundamental economic reforms in 4 "Ls": - Land, Labour, Liquidity and Laws. This is in line with the third revolution.

SKILLSertifika brings you a two-part series in form of two books to enable you to cope with this "ONCE-IN-A-CENTURY" challenge. The two books deal with four keywords: -

HOPE-RESILIENCE-THINKING-INNOVATION.

➤ *Hope leads to Resilience.*
➤ *Resilience leads to Thinking.*
➤ *Thinking leads to Innovation and great products.*

Why Innovation fails in most of the companies? because the first three elements go missing or not taken care of. This is our key hypothesis.

Our two-part series deals with this hypothesis. The first book – titled RESILIENCE deals with the first two elements of the hypothesis – Hope and Resilience. The second book titled: - COUNTER-INTUITIVE INNOVATION deals with the next two elements: - Thinking and Innovation.

In this book we have attempted to say three things: -

1. In the ensuing chapter we have explained what is the third economic revolution all about? What are its implications for society and business POST COVID 19?

2. Through a series of twelve gripping stories of man eater hunting, WW 2 and stories from Indian defence forces dating back to

'65 and '71 Indo-Pak conflict and an almost unbelievable story of courage of an Indian Navy Helicopter crew in 2017 we have enumerated twelve principles or the twelve knights of resilience: - how these twelve principles helps one find HOPE in difficult times.

3. In the last chapter we have collated the learnings from previous chapters to build a framework termed as COUNTER-INTUITIVE THINKING, the key to build resilience in difficult times at the backdrop of the third economic revolution.

4. **THIS IS THE KEY TAKEAWAY OF THE BOOK FOR MANAGERS, ACADEMIC SCHOLARS AND ANYONE WHO WANTS TO SUCCEED IN LIFE**

CHAPTER 2

The once in a century challenge

The old Phoenix has withered away and the new Phoenix has just risen from the ashes and peering around

Economic revolutions are never a result of technology alone. In late 1990s (1997 to be correct), the late Clayton Christensen published his now famous theory of Disruptive Innovation, which was mainly how an inferior and new technology goes on to become the dominant technology of the day, disrupting industries and reshaping them. While the role of the technology factor cannot be underestimated (as Tech 4.0 disrupts our lives in a big way today), disruptions are happening today beyond technology and on a wider and deeper scale.

Economic revolutions require two more elements: - a) a new business model b) a new enterprise structure and a set of practices that go with it.

The first economic revolution saw advent of steam-based technologies, transcontinental supply chains powered by the steam ship and telegraph and new organizational architectures in form of large Joint Stock Public corporations, whose shares were traded in stock exchanges. Advent of audit firms like Price-Waterhouse and Coopers & Lyband (Today's PWC) and advent of English Companies act – defining the joint stock corporation, which separated owner's liabilities from that of an enterprise – this fuelled the growth of 19th

century giants.

The second revolution was oil based. It saw advent of the aviation and automobile industry – two cornerstones of 20th century civilization, a new business model spanning multiple locations, based on "**Scale-Size-Standardization**" paradigm or the 3 S's. The 3 S's triggered the outsourcing wave in 1990s, based on theories of Transaction Cost Economics. The third element was the new form of enterprise – the multi-divisional organization, powered by new age management practices in accounting (the key metric – ROCE or return on capital employed and separation of fixed and variable costs, determining the contribution margin). Much later the multi divisional form evolved into today's giant matrix organizations.

The second revolution has run its course! The third revolution commenced sometime in 2010's, the second decade of this century and in last 10 years have gained momentum. Joseph Schumpeter's theory of Creative Destruction (unfortunately) is in full swing (Lord Shiva's dance of destruction as per Indian Mythology) and by 2030 will peak, leaving a trail of destruction in its wake. The oil revolution destroyed a bevy of 19th century industries such as Gas Lamps and Horse Carriages and artisan-based industries were destroyed by the mass production paradigm, which could produce a good at $1/10^{th}$ of the previous cost. A hand-crafted automobile costed $ 3000 onwards in early 20th century – a fortune in those days, putting the car beyond the reach of the masses. Henry Ford brought down the cost to just $ 250 by 1920s with his Model-T, triggering the automobile revolution.

History is repeating itself and those who forget history are condemned to repeat it.

So today disruptions are happening in three spheres simultaneously: -

  a) Technology
  b) Business Model
  c) Organization structure and practices

And together they constitute the third economic revolution, already on its way and gathering momentum day by day.

Energy-Communication Matrix

As explained in introduction, economic revolutions are powered by three main forces – a) the changing customer habits b) new business models and c) new enterprise structures. However, if one looks deeper: - there lies something even more fundamental! The changing energy and communication matrix, which triggers economic revolutions. The first matrix was steam-telegraph in 19th century, which was the foundation of the first revolution. The second was the oil-wireless matrix, later on further enhanced by the automobile and aircraft, powering the oil- based revolution and the third matrix is shaping up right in front of our eyes. It's the renewable energy-internet matrix, which will result in SMART power grids. The cost of communication has already fallen dramatically triggering the social media emergence, however the connecting part: - cheaper energy is yet to happen, blocked as it is by the oil lobby and still higher installation and maintenance costs of renewable energy sources and lack of e-mobility in form of charging stations across the globe, which can fuel the growth of e-vehicles, backed by SMART grids and the third matrix will fuel the growth of SMART cities.

How the world Post Covid-19 may look like?

There are a number of possible scenarios: -

a) Small will appear big through a network, the David can upturn a Goliath through the power of a network! Individual size, scale will no more provide barriers to entry.

b) Social capital and intangible knowledge assets will play a greater role than financial capital and physical assets.

c) The era of single or dual core competencies are over. A firm must build up multiple core competencies to deliver platforms, bundling products with services and combining digital power. This challenges the notion of related and unrelated diversifications – a notion held dear for more than half a century.

d) Increasing customer power will force many companies to be transparent and honest in their offerings. For example – does a toothpaste really kill germs? Does a health drink really contain the nutrients as claimed by the firm? Does a car weigh as much as the auto maker claims and develop as much engine power or the battery of the e-vehicle lasts as many kilometres on a single charge as claimed?

e) The era of "Me-Too" products based on cost is over. Its unique products with a DEEP IMPACT – which influences people's lives significantly (WALKMAN) will be commonplace. Hence a firm who can deliver a WALKMAN time and again will flourish. We are entering an era of "Innovation for Greater Good" from an era of "Innovate to Compete". Every firm will have to find a higher purpose, beyond profits and provide a far higher degree of value addition. If one can deliver a DEEP IMPACT product, profits will anyway follow. The very definition of competition and strategy may undergo a paradigm shift with such Deep Impact products/services.

f) An era of Collaborations may dawn on us. If the past century was an era of competition this century post Covid-19 may well be an era of collaborations, spanning over digital networks

g) We may witness a greater degree of transparency, empathy and honesty in corporate-customer interactions. Today a number of Pharma Companies are collaborating together to bring out a vaccine for Covid-19. What may have normally taken five years for one single company is being attempted to be accomplished by a number of companies together within next five to seven months. This also may well imply that rogue businesses who thrived by cheating customers may not survive in a post Covid-19 era. Availability of information will force many companies to junk past dishonest practices. For example, a company selling non vegetarian products may be forced to disclose how it treats animals and how the meat is sourced.

However, one word may ring through all efforts to bring back the global economy – RESILIENCE. Resilience to survive, resilience to weather the uncertainty, resilience to win the customer over, resilience to innovate novel products and services for greater good, resilience to bring back the national economies on their feet.

The key to framing a strategy in uncertain times is to ask a set of ten relevant questions today:

1. What business are we in?

2. What new competences can we build?

3. What was good and is no longer good?

4. What practices will become irrelevant very soon?

5. What unexpected events to expect?

6. Who are not our customers?

7. What are the key strategic risks that can hit us hard and cripple us?

8. How to build technology-human interfaces?

9. Where we need to take a more than calculated risk?

10. What is the bigger cause or purpose that will propel us through the adversity?

(This entire chapter has been adapted from a published paper in FORESIGHT, a refereed academic journal of Emerald publishers, titled: "The March Towards Infinity" by Dr. S Dasgupta and Debashis Sanyal. Jan-2020.)

CHAPTER 3

Resilience - Making the impossible happen

You will walk through the dark fires of hell Charred and Shining

Resilience is anticipating the unexpected and being prepared for it, being willing to face the uncertainty, risk, hardship and emerge triumphant, as the following stories narrate. There are situations, where something more is demanded of the person beyond years of training, experience and knowledge. That something more is the will to take great risks, a will to go through the fires of hell and survive – take a decision that defies logic and is fuelled by a desire to save lives – to bring smiles on faces, to bring victory to the nation. We sifted through numerous man-eater hunting and war stories to pick twelve stories of extraordinary courage in face of adversity, facing the heaviest odds and emerging triumphant.

These twelve stories have a common thread running through them – displaying an unusual combination of sixth sense and courage, combined with years of training, skill and experience – **and the facts defy common sense or logic, in every case success seemed impossible!**

Thus, the wisdom and the lessons that these twelve stories teach can be termed counter-intuitive and has immense potential for applications in business field, to innovate for a bigger purpose. Four of them are stories of man-eater hunting by two famed hunters –

Jim Corbett in Kumaon and Kenneth Anderson in Southern India. Two of them are stories of grit and resilience from the annals of World Cup football. The other five are war stories, two of them of the Indian army and the air force, while three relate back to WW II. The last story is a hard to believe story of an Indian Navy helicopter crew, on a mission to save lives. Each of them teaches us a lesson in counter-intuitive wisdom, that the impossible can be possible and the unimaginable can happen.

These twelve Counter-Intuitive lessons are especially relevant during these times of tumultuous change with the third economic revolution peaking and COVID-19 crisis accelerating it.

1. Find a bigger purpose and you can overcome the greatest stress to accomplish it

1929 April. Jim Corbett was directing an elephant mounted hunt for birds, wild-boar and deer. There were more than 10 shooters mounted with different guns on 10 or 15 elephants. An accidental discharge of a powerful rifle next to his left ear, singed his inner ear drum. Abscesses started forming in his head. The hospital ear surgeon in Nainital informed him that nothing can be done. This was a time; antibiotics were not invented. There were two maneaters menacing the lives of people in Kumaon – the Talladesh man eating tigress and the Chowgarh tigress. Off to Talladesh Corbett went ignoring all protests!

He arrived in Talladesh region after walking for days and witnessed three mysterious lights on the peaks above the Purnagiri Temple on the way. He was told that he is the first European to witness the lights – it's the spirit of a saint who worships the Goddess Bhagwati and only when one is on a very difficult and noble mission – one is accorded the privilege of seeing the lights. This privilege was accorded to him by the Goddess because he was on a mission to save lives.

He arrived in a village named Tallakote. Shortly after his arrival he was informed by the villagers that three tigers are sunning themselves in a valley below the village! It was the man-eating tigress and her two cubs. With his 7 mm (0.275 caliber) Mauser Rigby, he shot the cubs with two bullets and severely injured the tigress with the third. The tigress was lying unconscious stuck on a sapling. After a few seconds it fell from the sapling and rolled down the grassy slope of the hill. Corbett fired a fourth one on the rolling tigress and missed. All thought that the tigers are dead! People started dancing with joy!

Suddenly the tigress got up and started running! A boy detected the parting of the grass and the tigress through it and pointed out – look Sahib the tigress is running away! Corbett had last one bullet in the magazine of his rifle and the distance was 500 yards – just within the range of this light rifle, as he was asked by the doctor to not to use his heavy 11/10 mm (0.450/0.400 caliber) double barreled rifle. He fired and missed. He regretted the fourth shot – which he fired in sheer joy, when the tigress was rolling down the grassy slope! IT WAS MATTER OF ONE BULLET TO FINISH THE TALE. WHICH WAS NOT TO BE!! His sufferings had just begun.

Corbett chased the tigress up and low in the valleys of Talladesh for next five days. His miseries kept increasing as the Abscess kept becoming worse. By fifth day evening the abscess grew very big. Blocked and closed his left eye, immobilized his left shoulder, he couldn't move his neck to left. His left ear drum was destroyed. The abscess practically immobilized his left side! Last 48 hours he chased the tigress living on a diet of milk-based tea! On fifth day evening after chasing the tigress for 18 hours that day, he decided that the night is the do-or-die moment to settle scores with the tigress, who has killed 150 people and if she recovers from her injuries, she will kill more. He walked in to the jungle in a moonlit night. His six Garhwali servants standing and crying.

He was resting for a while under an oak tree, when he spotted the tigress 150 yards to his left. Corbett started running with his head bent. Was overcome with vertigo. His head started spinning. There was an oak tree nearby. He climbed the oak tree and not knowing what to do just sat down with his head buried in his hands. At that moment the abscess burst! "No greater joy is known to man with the sudden caseation of pain" – writes Corbett. It was midnight. He lay asleep on the tree. Woke up at dawn to see that his left eye was open, he was free to move his neck and he was well! That day morning, he came face to face with the tigress and put two bullets in her head to finish the tale [1].

1: - adapted from The Talladesh Maneater in The Temple Tiger Oxford University Press. India. 1997

2. A chance however forlorn should be taken and a greater sense of purpose can help taking difficult decisions, miracles may happen!

Jim Corbett's last man eater hunt was the Thak maneater in 1938. He was 63 then. By then he had added 32 years of man eater hunting experience and shot more than ten, man eaters. Yet this tigress troubled him to no end and he said: - "I would exchange all my thirty-two years of man eater hunting experience to take that one unhurried shot at the tigress". He searched the tigress high and low through the hills and ravines of Thak village in Kumaon region of Uttarakhand state in India for days and couldn't even see a breadth of her hair. This shrewd tigress eluded him till the last day of his man eater hunting. Corbett writes: - "this was my last day of man eater hunting and it's hard to describe the depression that assails a man on failure and yet I feel there is nothing that I left undone". As he wearily trudged down the hill path, he heard the tigress call a few hundred yards down to his left in a deep ravine full of thick forest. It was 5 pm in the evening and the Sun was casting a red glow on the Nepal Himalayas, darkness would descend in another thirty minutes. He had four men and two goats following him.

He understood that this was a mating call and the man-eating tigress is searching for a mate. Corbett was an expert in imitating a tiger's call and he faced a life challenging dilemma: - to call or not to call? He had about thirty minutes to complete the task. If he called and the tigress came, he can put a pair of bullets from his double barrelled 0.450/400 Jeffries and end the miseries of hill people. But what if the tigress didn't show up? Once darkness descended, five men and two goats had to cross two miles of thick forest and one or more of them may not reach the safety of the camp! What should he do? Call or not call?

Corbett decided to call! What outweighed the sense of imminent danger was the consideration that if he went away listening the call, chose safety of five men over thousands of hill folk – that regret he will live with for rest of his life! Once he called, the tigress responded immediately and she was on her way to find her prospective mate! Corbett had less than 15 minutes now to position himself appropriately to hide himself behind a rock and keep calling and lure the tigress to her end. Seconds before darkness descended the tigress walked up the hill path and came face to face! Two shots rang out from the heavy double barrelled 0.450/0.400 rifle through the hills [2].

2: - adapted from the Thak Maneater in Maneaters of Kumayun. Oxford University Press. India, 1997.

3. Think like a Tiger to Hunt Him! The element of Slow thinking

Like Corbett in Kumaon, there was an equally daring hunter who shot more than 50-man eaters in Southern India – a Scotsman called Kenneth Anderson. Anderson's tales span from late 30s to 60s. He worked in HAL factory in Bengaluru and hunted around the jungles, now part of Mudumalai, Nagarhole, Bandipur reserve. Once he was with two forest rangers in a bungalow. It was dark by the time the meeting ended. The rangers warned: - there is a man-eating tiger prowling around! He should better spend the night in the lodge. Anderson had his trusted 0.405 (10 mm) Winchester with him and a torch was attached on the rifle's barrel. It was a single barreled rifle with 5 bullets in magazine. He refused and started his walk towards his bungalow – 6 kms away thru thick forest. After a couple of kilometers his sixth sense – honed by years of hunting (and being hunted!) started warning him!! The maneater is stalking him! Yet the jungle was silent. No alarm calls of deer. The wind was not blowing, everything was ominously silent. Yet Anderson was sure! The tiger is stalking him! He had to stop panicking and, in this situation, THINK SLOWLY. He had to fight the natural response when you are stalked by a man-eating tiger in a thick forest – RUN FOR YOUR LIFE OR CLIMB A TREE OR FIRE THE BULLET TO DRAW THE TIGER OUT. No! he had to do something different! Anderson thought carefully. He stood for a minute on the forest path thinking. What is a Tiger's instinct? He is the king of the forest! He is accustomed to roar and chase his victims! He is accustomed to see his victims cry and shriek in fright! This natural tendency of a Tiger has to be used against this man eater! Anderson looked around and saw a small hillock ahead. He made up his mind! The plan was to run like a victim and climb the hillock fast, with the rifle ready to fire and the torch switched on. He did just that! He ran hard, with a cocked rifle and torch on! The tiger was ACTUALLY THERE! He roared out of the bushes and chased him. It was a question of WHO RAN FASTER! Anderson fortunately reached the hillock and turned around just in time to focus the torch on tiger's snarling face with open teeth. The heavy 0.405 Winchester bullet crashed into the tiger's nose while he was just two feet away. He fired again! It misfired!! It was fortunate that the first bullet in the magazine was a good round, otherwise the tiger would have completed his attack. He reloaded and fire a third round; the tiger had vanished with the injury by then. [3]

3: - adapted from: - 'Sher Khan and the Betamugalam Man Eater' The Kenneth Anderson Omnibus. Vol.2. Rupa & Co. 2006

4. Combine Insanity with Logic

Kempekerai is a small hamlet in north Salem district of Tamil Nadu and in late 30s was menaced by a man eater. Anderson was summoned to get rid of the menace. He first sat on a tree. Missed shooting the tiger. Then he had a crazy, but workable idea: - tracing the tiger's tracks he chose a dry stream to fix a dummy on one bank of the stream, dig a hole in the stream, ask his helpers to secure the hole with a bullock cart wheel with heavy stones placed on it! Keep a six-inch hole under the wheel open to aim at the dummy and fire when the tiger pounces on the dummy! A crazy and brave idea indeed. The plan didn't work out the way Anderson hoped. The Tiger didn't come from the direction he expected. A bear came before him and discovered Anderson's position and snooped around. The resulting noise alerted the tiger and he approached the hole carefully to investigate. He discovered Anderson and nearly killed him! It only shows how carefully thought out plans can go haywire! In sheer panic Anderson somehow managed to touch the tiger's shoulder with the barrel of his 0.405 Winchester and the bullet smashed the tiger's left shoulder from close quarters, saving Anderson's life. But as Anderson sat in the whole wondering what next, drops of rain water started falling and soon he heard a torrent rushing down from the nearby hillock! It was a flash flood and Anderson risked the danger of being drowned alive! With great difficulty he extricated himself from the hole, now a death trap and ran out. Seventeen days later, he traced the severely injured tiger's tracks on the Chinar river and spotted a stone in middle of the river. They were fresh. The tiger was around! His pugmarks showed that he was severely injured on the left side and unable to place his foot. Result of the heavy 0.405 bullet damaging his left shoulder and feet seventeen days back.

He conjured another insanely brave plan! Sat on top of the stone, dressed as a farmer. A torch attached to his Winchester. Around eleven he noticed a faint dark shape on the left-hand side about a hundred yards away! Strange! He thought. That shape was not there before! Then it suddenly became elongated and again shortened! Anderson understood! The tiger has spotted him and is reducing the distance slowly, before launching the final charge. He started shivering and perspiring and understood that being afraid will not help! THIS WAS THE MOMENT OF RESILIENCE AND COURAGE. He switched on the torch beam and it revealed the snarling face of the man eater. Three shots rang out. [4]

4: - adapted from "The Marauder of KempeKerai" Kenneth Anderson Omnibus Vol1. Rupa & co. 2001.

5. Challenge the default and think what can go wrong – the positive power of negative thinking!

Euro 2000 was football powerhouse Germany's lowest point as they were eliminated in the group stage itself, failing to advance to the knockouts. This is German football's nadir – poor performance, a very poor team and poor management – stated Rafael Honigstein to CNN. From the low of 2000 to world cup victory in 2014 in Brazil against Lionel Messi's feared Argentinians – the team that was expected to win the cup, with the World's no.1 ranked footballer in charge of the team, beating a Latin American team in the mecca of football: - the Maracanã stadium in Rio De Janeiro and in the process becoming the first European team to win the world cup in Latin America, beating the two giants of world football: - Brazil 7-1 and Argentina 1-0, the German football team rewrote history. How did they do it?

The real changes came in 2004. The first was a youth development program – in 366 centres, unearthing young and talented footballers and building up the bench strength, so that if the frontline footballer gets injured as the tournament progresses, the bench strength can take over and the final great moment of German football came in last seven minutes of a 120 minute nail biting game against a tough opponent comprising some of the world's top rated footballers at that time, when the goal was scored by two substitutes. One passed and another scored! The bench strength demonstrates think what can go wrong and be prepared! On the day of final, Sami Khedira, the most influential player in the middle was out of contention. His replacement Christoph Kramer had to be replaced during the match, his replacement Andre Schurrle provided the winning pass and the goal was scored by Mario Goetze, who came in as a substitute in 88th minute in place of the most experienced striker Miroslav Klose!

However, the bigger change was in the philosophy of German football. From being efficient, doing the essential, focusing on speed, stamina, passing and group game – a new philosophy was adapted which combines virtues of the old system with individual skill. The world cup winning German team's coach Joachim Loew came as assistant coach under Juergen Klinsmann in 2004 and was immediately involved in changing the playing style of the team – combining flair with team work and stamina. The result was talented strikers like Thomas Mueller, who could appear like a ghost in the opponent penalty box to score (and played a major role in Germany's 2014 story) and Bastian Schweinsteiger – who controlled the midfield and Phillip Lahm – one of the most versatile full-backs global football has seen in recent times. Another vital factor was allowing immigrant footballers to come up. The German team in 2014 had talented immigrant footballers like Mesut Ozil, Gerome Boateng and Sammy Khedira.

Thus, Loew and Klinsmann challenged the default and let go of past. They forged a totally different looking German team in 2014 – in fact it did appear that Germany was playing like great Brazilian teams of past and Brazil was attempting to play like German teams of past after their 1-7 defeat.

But there was much more to the tale of 10 years of preparation under two men – Loew and Klinsmann. Germany was in a tougher group, then Argentina with Portugal, USA and Ghana – all good teams and Portugal itself was one of the strong contenders of the cup with another footballing great – Christiano Ronaldo at the helm, who was rated as one of the top two footballers in European club football and shared the dais of honour with Messi. Germany smashed Portugal with a shock 4-0 victory, drew 2-2 with the talented and young Africans, who really challenged them and managed to beat a tough and defensive USA 1-0 to progress to knockouts.

One surprise feature was – one heard very little from the team's management or barely saw the players celebrating after every match. There were no negative or controversial reports in media and the German team remained in isolation, going back to the training after every match and as the tournament progressed, they became better and better with focus, teamwork, focusing on what can go wrong and choking the opponent with surprise moves. The key players making surprise moves were Lahm at the back and Schweinsteiger, Khedira at the middle – while Mueller often surprised the opponent by appearing out of nowhere. Mueller reminds us of another two German footballing greats of 70s – Gerard Mueller and Frantz Beckenbauer, who won the World cup for Germany in 1974, against a great Holland Team which had Johann Cruyff – nicknamed Flying Dutchman. This is still rated as one of the best world cup football finals till date, in which Germany (then West Germany) won a nerve wracking final 2-1.

40 years after the 2014 team was attempting to repeat history against another footballing great of our times – Lionel Messi.

After 90 minutes of nerve wracking and brilliant football, it was extra time and this was the moment Loew's team waited for 24 years since Lothar Matheus's team won the world cup in 1990 against another Argentine Legend – Maradona's team who won the previous cup. It was a question of COLLECTIVE RESILIENCE, a brush at destiny, a supreme test of will to live a historic moment and they were not going to let it go! Two young substitutes did it! With barely seven minutes to go of extra time, Andre Schurrle, who was the second substitute picked up the ball on left wing, just across the midfield. With three opponents in front, he decided to be positive and run with the ball. Spotted a small gap and he sped past a maze of blue shirts, nearing the touchline. When almost near the touchline with Argentine defenders threatening to snatch the ball and forcing it out of play, he crossed the ball spotting a white shirt. That white shirt was Mario Gotze, one of the seven Bayern Munich players, in his early twenties and was barely 25 minutes old in the match (88th -113th)! Gotze didn't lose his nerves! He instinctively thought what can go wrong! Soft chested the ball to control it and then barrelled it across with a powerful left volley. The ball flew into the far side of the net and history was created once more![5]

5: - *Adapted from the following websites: -*

https://www.livemint.com/Specials/V9y68aRPPg2axLuhut5KiO/Five-reasons-why-Germany-won-the-World-Cup.html

http://edition.cnn.com/2014/07/15/sport/football/world-cup-final-germany-argentina-reasons-for-success/index.html

https://en.wikipedia.org/wiki/2014_FIFA_World_Cup_Final

6. Underdogs and misfits will often do things no one else can think of! – The story of the little country with big dreams – Croatia, 2018 world cup football finalist

After rewriting history in 2014, Germany made a quiet exit from the next world cup in Russia. By then some of its footballing greats like Schweinsteiger had retired. Many of the stalwarts of the 2014 team were no more. But the 2018 world cup soccer will be remembered for rise of one team – an underdog, who did unexpected things and played extra ordinary football till the end and succumbed to injuries in final, losing to a fitter and more energetic French team, but not going down before scoring two goals, eventually going down 4-2. It did appear in the end that the Croatians were exhausted, outrun by their younger opponents. However, when one thinks of European football, one thinks of Germany, Italy, France, Holland and Belgium – the top five teams and three of them have won the cup more than once, producing some of the legendary footballers over the years. At the commencement of the cup, no expert ever thought of an Eastern European nation playing some extraordinarily brilliant football to reach the finals beating giants along the way.

Prior the tournament, the impression was that global football was in the grip of a few rich European nations, with strong club and talent nurturing systems and a few football crazy Latin American nations and its these nations who regularly featured as finalists. 2018 changed all that! There were a series of upsets and the previous world cup finalists didn't make it to the last four. A little and unknown Eastern European country challenged every dearly held notion of world football. Croatia eventually lost and clearly looked an exhausted side with 4 goals conceded and players playing with injuries as the average age of the team was nearly 30 and it was one of the oldest teams age wise in the tournament and by the team they reached the final, many of the key players were nursing injuries, they lacked the bench strength of 2014 Germany, the economics of a small country didn't allow the luxury of 366 centres grooming young footballers and against a strong and young French side the odds were heavily stacked against them.

But they left the tarmac with heads held high, not disgraced in defeat, drawing appreciation from all quarters and most important – left a strong message – YOU NEED NOT BE RICH TO MAKE YOUR MARK IN THE WORLD'S MOST PLAYED SPORT: - FOOTBALL, where nearly 160 countries compete once in four years to reach the final 32. This comes from a country that never made it to the last 16 since 1998. Although from time to time Croatia has produced talented players who individually made their mark in European club football, however they never gelled as a great side producing magic.

Zlatko Dalic wanted to change all that. He had a conundrum to resolve: - to harness the individual play making skills of two of his most talented players: - Luka Modric and Ivan Rakitic. Modric traditionally played from the deep, rising from the deep, combining defensive play with attack. Players in front of him rarely provided great passes and Croatia often charged down the flanks with Modric leading, while its talented mid-field comprising Rakitic, Brozovic and Kovacic contributed little. Dalic, pushed Modric up, making him wear the legendary no.10 jersey! Now Rakitic was behind, this move made Modric see less of the ball with less time up in front to charge ahead. He was now depending on Rakitic to pass on the ball. This was a game changer! Modric went onto play the greatest tournament of his life and take his team to final.

Croatia has relied on strength of mind to overcome the disadvantage of limited resources and became the smallest nation in 68 years, since Uruguay in 1950 to reach final. The high point: - the underdogs thrashing Messi's Argentina 3-0!

What was the key? Croatia knew they are underdogs. THEY WILL HAVE TO TRY HARDER THAN NORMAL, HARDER THAN ANYONE ELSE. The 32-year-old Modric till final ran 63 kms on turf! He ran harder than anyone else! He was all over the field, egging on his team mates and passing on the ball constantly. Modric was awarded the GOLDEN BALL award: - Man of the Tournament for his stellar role in Croatia reaching the finals.

Till they reached the final, Croatia came back to win four matches from being down with a goal, winning two penalty shootouts and three extra time matches, beating Denmark, Russia and England on the way in knockouts.

Croatian team left a strong message – one can overcome all one's drawbacks and make an impression, if one is willing to. It's not talent, it's not money, privilege, power, position or anything else – JUST THE WILL TO SUCCEED AND THE WILL TO NOT GIVE UP.

Both the world cup football stories demonstrate this. [6]

6: - adapted from the following websites: -

https://www.independent.co.uk/sport/football/world-cup/world-cup-final-2018-france-croatia-zlatko-dalic-luka-modric-what-we-learned-a8449421.html

https://www.theguardian.com/football/2018/jun/05/croatia-world-cup-2018-team-guide-tactics-key-players-luka-modric-zlatko-dalic

https://www.firstpost.com/sports/fifa-world-cup-2018-croatias-dejan-lovren-points-to-teams-mental-strength-as-one-of-the-key-factors-behind-successful-run-4732901.html

https://edition.cnn.com/2018/07/13/football/croatia-world-cup-france-final-russia-2018-spt-int/index.html

7. Under extreme adversity, fired by a sense of great purpose, a team together can produce a collective resilience, which is hard to match

Dec 19th, 1944. Bastogne, Belgium. The town was covered in white, temperature minus 20 degrees centigrade. There were fifteen SS divisions surrounding the town. Facing them was the 101st and 82nd airborne paratrooper division of the US army. A few days back the Nazis launched a surprise and unexpected offensive in Belgium, the aim – to reach the port of Antwerp and capture it, which was the supply life line of the allies for invasion in Europe. Hitler's plan was to capture the port and force the allied commanders into negotiation, reaching an honourable face off and cease hostilities. The German troops faced the paratroopers in the town of Bastogne and surrounded them. Bad weather ensured no air attacks could be launched by the allies – which Hitler knew.

To stop the Nazi advance, Eisenhower – the supreme commander of allied army rushed the paratroopers in trucks nonstop. He mastered over 11000 trucks. But the supplies were insufficient. Insufficient ammunition, food, medicines and winter clothing. Eisenhower didn't have enough time to build the supply lifelines, taken by surprise as he was like everyone else by Hitler! The fact that being on the backfoot Hitler could launch an offensive like this was unthinkable to Montgomery and Eisenhower – the two allied commanders! The Germans were in retreat since the D-day landing in Normandy, France, June 6, 1944 and this was December and the allied troops were already in France and in Holland advancing across Belgium to Germany, hoping to cross the Rhine by Christmas of 1944 and end the war by reaching Berlin! The allied army was in a state of advance and Hitler's sudden offensive took the Americans by surprise! Rushing the paratrooper divisions was an emergency measure to stop the German advance and preventing them from capturing the port of Antwerp.

The concept of a paratrooper with special training in fighting under extreme adverse circumstances came from these two US army divisions and became the global standard for special forces. Much later on came the Sayaret Matkal (Israel), Spetznaz (Russia), SAS (British), Green Berets. Navy Seals (USA) and in India the Para SF regiment – which has been instrumental in combating terrorism in Kashmir. The US army fielded 89 divisions on June 6, 1944 Normandy France – D-Day. Of these two were paratrooper divisions. The 82nd and the 101st airborne. A total of around twenty-two thousand specially trained men. They were the first to land in

France, airdropped by the DC 3 Dakotas much before the D-Day. Their task was to neutralize the German resistance before the main invasion force landed. They partially succeeded, dropped as they were in disparate locations and many lost their lives even before they touched the ground from heavy fire.

The two paratrooper divisions faced fifteen enemy units. The biggest enemy was not the Germans! It was the cold. The paratroopers were under-clothed, without winter clothing at minus twenty degrees and they froze, many incurred frost bites and suffered attacks of hypothermia. To add to their miseries, they were underfed, living on corn soup packets and melting ice to drink water, they were also without inadequate medical aid and many died after being injured by German artillery and mortar fire in absence of adequate Medicare. To add to their final tally of miseries, they were underarmed! Not enough bullets and shells to put on enemy! The supply lines were cut. Air dropping of supplies were not possible due to bad weather and ground supply lines were cut by surrounding Germans.

Hungry, under armed, inadequately clothed, the paratroopers dug in their fox holes. Every man knew he could depend on the man next to him and the man behind him. They made every bullet count and the Germans dared not launch infantry attacks, knowing they will be torn to shreds by accurate firing, every bullet will find its mark! Instead the Germans resorted to heavy shelling and at times the shells landed in foxholes straight!

It was the hell week. In words of Eugene the medic (Eugene was vividly portrayed in the 10-part HBO serial Band of Brothers, in the Bastogne episode) –After Christmas the skies cleared a bit allowing airdrop of supplies and in the new year General Patton's third army broke through the German lines to provide relief (7).

Courage, comradeship, idealism and training produced a resilience that Nazi Germany couldn't crack! This was the decisive turning point of the WW II, the paratroopers were the first to reach Eagle's nest in June 1945, ending the war in Europe. [7]

7: Adapted from "Band of Brothers" by Stephen E Ambrose. Chapter 11: - "They got us Surrounded. Bastogne. Dec 19-31, 1944". Simon & Schuster. 2001.

8. Every advantage has a corresponding disadvantage

September 8-10, 1965. 350 Pakistani Patton tanks stormed the Indian border as part of Operation Gibraltar. Their aim – cut off J&K from India and march towards Delhi on the GT road. They were overly sure of their victory after capture of the town of Khem Karan on Sept 5. they had intelligence information: - only 135 Indian tanks of the 2nd and 3rd cavalry. Many of the tanks were 1950s vintage – British Shermans. Only the 3rd cavalry had contemporary tanks – Centurions, which matched the Pattons. The Pakistanis were 150% sure of victory, the Patton was portrayed by the US Army as an invincible tank. They failed to take into account one factor – skill of Indian gunners and resolve of the 4th Grenadiers, who guarded the road to Delhi, the Pathankot highway! The Indian tanks formed a horse shoe shaped formation around a Sugar cane field. The tanks were hiding behind tall sugarcane plants. On the night of Sept 7, Brigadier Theograj made his soldiers dig up part of the sugarcane field, slush it up with mud and cover it expertly with grass. On the morning of Sept 8, more than 150 enemy tanks straight drove over the field and the heavier and bigger American made Pattons got stuck in the slush! THEY WERE NOW SITTING DUCKS! Not one Pakistani tank went back. Ayub Khan's dream of riding into the Red fort on a Patton remained a pipe dream. The Indian gunners made every shell count and Lt. Abdul Hameed single handedly shot 7 tanks before dying, he was awarded a posthumous PVC. Over optimism doesn't always pay – think out what can go wrong! [8]

8: Adapted from Wikipedia. The battle of Asal Uttar, Sept 8 to 10, 1965.

9. Have faith when you are up to something big and don't underestimate the role of providence!

September 1940. Europe was under Hitler's command. Only one country stood up against Hitler – England. The German ambassador invited his British counterpart for a talk and honorable surrender in Berlin – to which the British ambassador declined. "Try and cross the channel and show us!" he commented. We shall flatten you with our 2500 planes – commented the German Ambassador!

"The numbers don't count! Your aircraft will run out of fuel over the English skies!" The fact that Luftwaffe bombers will run short of fuel over the English sky was well known by the Brits. Also, in the British arsenal was a superior fighter – the SPITFIRE. This Fighter was Britain's trump card and the Luftwaffe were not really aware of the capabilities of this fighter. The most famous air war in history was fought between June and September 1940 and is known as the BATTLE OF BRITAIN. The RAF had around 650 fighters. The Luftwaffe around 2500. But this huge numerical superiority didn't play out in Germany's favor, short as they were of the big four-engine bombers like the US B-17/24, which could travel long distances with heavy loads. Also, the Spitfire proved more than a match for the German Messerschmitt's in later part of the war – another factor the Luftwaffe grossly underestimated. Yet, in the initial phase of the war, it did appear that the Luftwaffe plans were working. The bombers concentrated on the air fields, attempting to bomb the RAF out on the tarmac and they were largely succeeding in their mission. The RAF's biggest problem was not aircraft shortage, BUT PILOTS. The RAF was desperately short of pilots, and a majority of the RAF pilots had inadequate hours of training on the Spitfire – that was another major problem and better trained Luftwaffe fighter pilots in their ME-109 Messerschmitt's were blowing up the poorly trained Spitfire pilots out of the sky. The war seemed to be going the Luftwaffe's way till providence stuck and the Air Marshall Dowding's one critical decision turned out to be a game changer.

There were strict orders issued to the Luftwaffe pilots to not resort to terror bombing – that is bombing of civilian establishments. The pilots were supposed to only focus on the enemy – not the civilians. This was in line with the generic Soldier's code of conduct observed by both sides (observed even today by all professional air forces, in 65 and 71 hostilities, neither the PAF nor the IAF ever resorted to terror bombing). One Luftwaffe bomber strayed during a night bombing raid. Lost its coordinates and was strafed by British anti-aircraft fire. In panic the pilots dropped the bombs on London and sped home. They were court-martialled next day, taken off duty. That night British bombers bombed Berlin in retaliation. Hitler swore to bomb England out of existence! Now the Luftwaffe was ordered to bomb British towns, especially London.

This left the RAF airfields relatively free of bombing and allowed a beleaguered RAF to regroup. Some older Hawker Hurricane pre-war planes were pressed into service, their task was to shoot down the bombers, while the Spits focused on the ME-109s. Air Marshall Dowding took another critical decision – allowing of nearly 200 Polish pilots, who fled Poland after Poland surrendered to Germany at the beginning of the war. These Poles were well trained.

Now the RAF counter attacked with bigger numbers and they waited till the bombers expended their bomb loads and were low on fuel, as well as the fighters after hovering up on bomber protection duty were low on fuel. The tables turned drastically. The experienced Polish pilots were blowing the Germans out of the sky along with their better trained British counterparts.

The battle was a stalemate, Hitler gave up, turned his attention to Russia and England remained intact. Four years later the English soil was the launchpad of allied army invasion forces into the D-Day, June 6, 1944 [9].

9: Adapted from the Movie: - "The Battle of Britain" Directed by Guy Hamilton, 1969.

10. Think like the 10th Man

The famed Israeli intelligence agency MOSSAD has a principle. To anticipate a situation on national security, a 10th man is empowered to challenge and contradict what 9 others are thinking – this is known as the 10th man principle. The Allied army launched operation MARKET GARDEN in summer of 1944. The idea was audacious – to airdrop 35,000 crack para units to capture and retain key bridges over Belgium, the 1 British armored division will follow. The first British 1 para unit and the earlier mentioned units of US army – the 82nd and the 101st were assigned the task. There was a fourth unit – the Polish para division, which was kept in reserve (as General Montgomery was averse to the Poles!). It was assumed that German resistance will be negligible and soon the allied forces will march into Germany. The war will be over by Christmas of 44. One intelligence officer contradicted the entire hypothesis and questioned the wisdom of keeping the Polish division in reserve. He was overruled. He WAS THE 10TH VOICE, IGNORED!

The British first para was the first to be paradropped over Holland on a sunny and clear day. No resistance was offered, but they were watched! As the first para advanced and entered Dutch villages they came under well directed and well camouflaged fire, taking them by surprise. Their American counterparts were not doing great either. Each of the three para units reached a bridge and held it, fervently praying that the British armor and heavy artillery reach to help them! They were facing heavy fire from the German Panzers, who had camouflaged themselves expertly under nooks and crannies in villages and were now directing murderous and accurate fire on the para units. The camouflaged Panzers were not spotted by recce planes flying over Dutch villages. However, one Spitfire flew close over the villages and took a series of photos. The British intelligence officer enlarged all the photos and one particular photo caught his attention – what looked like a lump hiding under a heap of straw! After a careful analysis he requested another recce flight by the RAF. This time the RAF pilot took better photographs and one photograph revealed a long object under a hay stack!

The intelligence officer understood what the hidden long object under the hay stack meant! It was the hidden barrel of a Panzer! The Panzers were hiding in every village, well camouflaged. The Germans knew about operation Market Garden – the ambitious plan to capture the Arnhem bridge and cross the Rhine to enter Germany to end the war before Christmas of '44. They didn't offer any resistance at para landings, instead they waited! Allowed the enemy to come in and ambushed! The 10th man understood the plan – his voice was ignored. Either the movement of British 1 Armored regiment or the presence of the additional Polish Para division could have altered the outcome. But that was not to be! What if the Polish Para unit was around? NO ONE KNOWS! [10]

10: Adapted from the Movie: "A Bridge Too Far" directed by Richard Attenborough. 1977.

11. More is not always better – often you can deliver a lot more with lesser resources, if you are willing to dare beyond the ordinary!

September 4-5, 1971. The IAF was given the mandate of obliterating the PAF over the eastern skies so that the army can march to

Dacca within 10 days and liberate east Pakistan to create a new nation – Bangladesh. The IAF had eleven squadrons placed around in West Bengal and Assam for the task comprising 3 GNATs, 4 HUNTERs and 3 MIG-21 squadrons. The MIGS were based in Tezpur and Guwahati. The Hunters in Hashimara and Bagdogra in West Bengal. And the GNATS were for air defense around Kolkata. There was one Canberra and a SU-7 Sukhoi squadron based in Gorakhpur used for night bombing. The IAF's mandate was to bomb the PAF out of existence. For two days – the IAF carried out relentless sorties to bomb the Tezgaon airbase near Dhaka, where the PAF Sabres were located. They couldn't accomplish their task. The range of the fighters were not enough to hang over the base and bomb and when the PAF planes took off to challenge the IAF, the fuel proved insufficient to stay on and bomb. After two days of relentless attacks the Tezgaon base was intact and the enemy was still capable of fighting! Time was running out for IAF. Only one option remained – that required daring skill and courage. To bomb the Tezgaon runway in night at supersonic speeds. At that speed in the night the PAF fighters will not have sufficient time to take off and challenge the enemy, neither the PAF's anti-aircraft guns can do anything in the darkness. A secret project of the IAF was to train ten MIG pilots in practicing runway bombing using 500-pound Russian Runway penetrator bombs. The idea was to come down diving from 15000 feet at speed of sound and exactly align the aircraft on the runway to drop and climb back – an operation that required precise mathematics and physics! This was the only chance!

The IAF swallowed the bait and the ten MIG pilots were asked on night of Sept 5 to go into the mission. Eight MIGs flew in the first mission headed by Wing Cdr. Vishnoi on the morning of Sept 6. The technique was to climb to 15000 feet, invert the aircraft, align it with the runway, roll back and dive at an angle of 35-37 degrees and increase the speed with the dive with the bomb sight pointed at end of the runway. At 4500 feet, release the bomb and climb up. At that height and at near supersonic speeds the anti-air craft fire was useless. It was actually an almost forgotten and not in anymore use technique called "Steep-Glide" bombing, used by the Ju-87 Stukas of the Luftwaffe during WW II and RAF Mosquitos. The enemy was left speechless in surprise.

They accurately bombed the runway and destroyed it. The PAF engineers immediately set off to repair the runway. Sept 7 between 8.00 am and 12.30 pm was declared a ceasefire time zone by the UN, so that stranded foreign journalists and delegates can be evacuated from the war zone. The ceasefire came into effect at 8 am. At six am, the PAF planned sorties to stop advance of the Indian army armored regiments. At 4 am morning the runway was repaired and the PAF pilots were ready. Precisely at that time they heard the roar of the MIG 21's Tumansky engine in the dark. A solo MIG-21 piloted by Flt.Lt. Manbir (Buzzy) Singh was diving at supersonic speed! The MIG correctly positioned itself over the Tezgaon runway and dropped two 500 kg bombs on the runway. The runway was shattered. The ceasefire came into effect at 8 am, the PAF couldn't take off and the Indian army tanks proceeded at an electric pace towards Dhaka! The FATE OF EAST PAKISTAN IS SEALED – commented Wing Cdr. Dilawar Hussain, the PAF airbase in charge.[11]

11: Adapted from the book: - "Eagles over Bangladesh" by Jagan Mohan & Sameer Chopra. Harper & Collins, India. 2013.

12. Follow the inner voice, it may defy logic yet a miracle may happen!

Dec 1, 2017 a cyclone named Okchi had stuck two days before. Cyclones are not common in the Arabian sea, like on the eastern shores of India and although the met department sounded out several warnings about the severity of the cyclone, hundreds of fishermen were out at sea. Partly due to the pressure to earn a living, partly due to the fact that cyclones were practically unknown in western India and Arabian sea.

On Dec 1 morning, the Indian Navy's INAS 336 squadron was busy, flying rescue missions and searching for missing fishermen using its helicopters from the Kochi naval base. Around 1 pm, Captain P Rajkumar in his Sea King anti-submarine helicopter was guided by a P-81 surveillance aircraft towards four stranded fishermen in middle of a raging storm. The P-81 guided by a set of surveillance radars and flying at 1000 feet could detect the capsized boat with pinpoint accuracy. The P-81 737 was fitted with sensors and radars, that could detect the smallest object floating on sea surface and its laser beams detected coordinates with unerring accuracy. By evening the SK 528 Sea King had completed its rescue mission of the day, sunlight faded away and Okchi was assuming a terrifying form, with winds howling, and the sea swelling. The P-81 went to its home base.

Everything demanded the day to be closed! Mission accomplished! Logic demanded that venturing out to the sea again was as good as hara-kiri. Yet something nagged Captain Rajkumar! He had a strange sense of foreboding, a strange feeling that there might be someone out there in this raging storm who needs help! His crew understood and didn't say a word. They were ready! SK 528 was refueled and ventured out into the raging storm in pitch darkness. Missing was the reassuring presence of the P-81 above, it was night and the horizon reference, where the sea blended with the sky to keep the altitude was not possible in darkness. Rain blocked the windscreen and the search light reflected was creating a flying hazard, blinding the crew.

There were no coordinates, now definite detection of survivors at sea by the unerring radars and sensors of the P-81, no news, just a nagging feeling! And Rajkumar knew the standard saying of the military – there's a thin line dividing a gallantry award and a court martial. And yet! He carried on – just guided by a strange feeling that someone out there needs help in this raging storm. In the pitch blackness it was nearly impossible to detect a survivor, SK 528's crew was hunting blind. They knew that there's every chance that they will fly past their objective. But they stayed on! Five pairs of eyes squinting in every direction.

The endless search continued for an hour. The winds were raging and howling and the waves were rising higher. It was becoming more difficult every second and SK 528's crew was on the point of giving it up when they heard it! It was a call from a 100,000-ton cargo ship – the Cosco Beijing a Maltese container ship, that was standing stationery 80 kms from the Kochi coast. They were communicating on the frequency of 156.8 megahertz, the common frequency for merchant vessels, commonly known as Channel 16. Captain Rajkumar had kept the VHF radios of the chopper tuned to this channel. Now the ship saw the Indian Navy chopper's search lights and was communicating! "Boat Capsize!" In came the message with a heavy Chinese accent over the radio. Through a series of messages SK 528's crew understood that the container ship has detected a loan capsized boat and is now pointing a laser beam to guide the chopper to the boat.

This was perhaps a superior force directing SK 528! Its crew risked everything and put their years of training into practice, guided by a strange premonition in near impossible conditions – that in this raging storm there is a life waiting to be rescued! And now the Maltese ship is confirming it! The massive merchant vessel couldn't rescue the survivor, owing its size in this storm. There was every chance that it would have knocked the fisherman over into the sea with its giant hull heaving up and down in a bobbing motion. It couldn't go near the boat, but its crew spotted the Indian Navy chopper and lost no time in communicating.

SK 528 detected the big ship and started circling round it to pick up the laser beam. This was a very difficult task in the storm, as the helicopter was losing power when banked at 30 degrees angle. Says Captain Rajkumar: "No one will fly this long in such conditions. We have been flying hands-on for 6 hours without auto-pilot. But in such missions its adrenalin that keeps you going AND ITS MIND OVER BODY".

For 10 to 15 minutes, SK 528 hovered over the big ship and kept circling, trying to detect the small green streak of light and couldn't detect it in the raging storm. At last by a sheer stroke of luck Lt. Cdr. Mayur Chauhan spotted the small green ray of light.

Being a submarine hunter, SK 528 was designed to hover over a spot for long periods, but not below 50 feet. But under such conditions NOTHING THAT THE TRAINING MANUALS SAID WERE APPLICABLE. It was a game of pure guts and skill. Captain Rajkumar brought the helicopter down to 20 feet. At that height there was a huge risk of a sea swell hitting the tail rotor of the chopper which would have been catastrophic. In pitch darkness the horizon reference was not there and bobbing up and down, with skill of the two pilots SK 528 kept dodging the swelling waves and searched for the capsized boat.

They at last spotted the boat. Its blue fiberglass hulls. The boat was overturned and a lone man was clinging to the boat with help of a rope. He looked almost dead and appeared to have given up on life. This was the supreme moment of flying! Captain Raj Kumar had to simultaneously do two things now: - a) keep an eye on his instruments to avoid the swell of the sea and keep control of the chopper and keep up the lifting power of the engines b) keep an eye on the fisherman to not lose sight of him. Says the captain – "I was at one moment looking at the instruments and the fisherman at the other moment, it was that sort of flying we were doing out there". The chopper now hovered over the boat with a shuddering vibrating through its fuselage at a dangerously low height over the raging storm and swelling waves.

Now a terrible dilemma presented itself: - captain Rajkumar understood that the fisherman is not in a position to grab a rescue rope with a hook, so that he can be pulled over by the machine operated winch. A diver has to be lowered on to the boat! The decision can go horribly wrong if there is an alarm in the cockpit, an engine oil lubricant light coming on, or the rescue winch not working properly or a severe cockpit vibration, as the chopper was already flying dangerously low just over the waves. If the diver is lowered and anything goes wrong, he has to abandon two lives at sea. It was a gut-wrenching moment. And yet when marine commando diver Deepak Saini said – "I will Go", the captain knew that the decision had to be taken. Says Saini: - "In that moment I knew I had to save the fisherman! In that moment you are not thinking about yourself. How can you? Here was an opportunity to save a life!"

Saini was lowered by the other marine diver on the boat with a green fluorescent light to keep track of both. First the fisherman was hooked on to the winch. Then Saini was taken up. The fisherman was clinging to the boat for three days without food and water, a supremely strong will to live kept him alive and a strange premonition on part of Captain Rajkumar, saved his life against heaviest odds.[12]

12: - adapted from the story: - "What's higher than saving somebody's life?" featuring Captain P. Rajkumar the Commander of SK 528 Sea King Helicopter. Indian Navy Anti-Submarine Unit. From the book "India's Most Fearless Vol. 2 by Shiv Aroor & Rahul Singh", Penguin Ebury Press, India. 2019.

CHAPTER 4

Build Resilience with Counter-Intuitive Thinking and Cross the Valley of Death

The Wicked Perish the Righteous Rises from the Ashes Like a Phoenix

Henry Ford once thought: what if the car was moving and workers were stationery, instead of workers moving and finishing the car stationery at one spot? As was the usual practice those days? And thus, was born one of the greatest management innovations of 20th century – the mass production paradigm, which changed the 20th century civilization and we all enjoy its benefits even today. The idea of making the worker stationery was paradoxical in those times and thinking beyond the ordinary – which no one is thinking.

We attempted to portray the "Once-In-A-Century" challenge in 2nd chapter and decided that times such as this requires THINKING BEYOND THE ORDINARY. As economies sink, businesses shut down, people lose their jobs, what will give the layman reader the most precious commodity in times of crisis – HOPE?

This book went in search of some original ideas, from gripping adventure tales. Of pitting one's skill and courage against a wily man-eater, of two football teams attempting to do something beyond the ordinary, of a paratrooper division specially trained to withstand adverse circumstances holding off a superior enemy with minimum resources. Of a bunch of MIG pilots delivering the coup-de-grace using a forgotten technique, of an Air-Marshall taking an unusual decision to allow foreign pilots to fly British aircraft, of a wily Indian army commander understanding and sensing the over-confidence of the enemy and using it to his advantage and above all after performing a successful rescue mission, with absolutely no reason to take off again into the darkness over a stormy sea – with no clues about what the hell he is doing and the fact that if his helicopter crashes or returns with a damage – he will face court martial, Captain Rajkumar still took off! Just a hunch, a premoni-tion – that there is a life waiting to be rescued out there! He over-came the heaviest odds to pull off an almost impossible mission. The German team always thought of what can go wrong and they used the positive power of negative thinking and challenged the default to create history, the Croatian team followed an underdog strategy and despite being the oldest team in the tournament they ran all over the field! Luka Modric was awarded the golden ball – and he was not supposed to be in possession of the ball much wearing the no.10 jersey! He ran 63 kms on the field at the age of 32, 22.7 without the ball to win the golden ball award!

Modric perhaps best demonstrates the key lesson this book at-tempts to draw from these twelve stories – King Arthur's twelve knights: - THE ELEMENT OF COUNTER INTUITION. The fact that he wearing the no.10 jersey was not supposed to be in possession of the ball much and yet went on the win the award is counter intui-tive! He followed a hard strategy – run and run! In fact the entire Croatian team overcame every drawback to pit their minds over physical disabilities of age, lack of resources, lack of bench strength to follow an unusual strategy to create history and they will no doubt continue to inspire smaller and unknown footballing nations in future – that it is possible to beat the giants, it need not be a Ger-many/Italy/Brazil/Argentina every time winning the cup. France it-self won the cup after 20 years since 1998.

Let's put the twelve lessons in one place for you to understand the element of counter intuition better: -

1. Find a bigger purpose and you can overcome the greatest stress to accomplish it

2. A chance however forlorn has to be taken and a greater sense of purpose can enable one to arrive at difficult decisions

3. Think like the tiger to hunt him – think slow!

4. Combine insanity with logic

5. Challenge the default and think of the negatives – the positive power of negative thinking

6. Underdogs and misfits will often do things no else can will think of

7. Collective resilience fired by a sense of purpose is hard to beat

8. Every advantage has a corresponding disadvantage

9. Have faith when you are up to something big

10. Think like the 10th man

11. Often you can deliver a lot more with lesser resources and at times additional resources don't always help

12. Follow your inner voice – it may defy logic! Yet a miracle may happen

Now let us understand the VALLEY OF DEATH situation through a metaphor

Say a bird which was born in a large cage, grew up flying around the cage and used to being fed at regular intervals with food and water suddenly one day finds the door of the cage open and the food and water supply has stopped. The bird has two options: - a) step out of the cage into the strange and unfamiliar world, fly over the city to find a safe tree or a park where there are a number of trees and other birds of its type, insects and fruit as food and a pond in middle of the park. Alternately, if there is a forest nearby fly into the forest b) stay in the cage waiting for food and water to arrive, which may never arrive and other hand a cat may enter the cage to kill and eat it.

The third economic revolution combined with the current Covid-19 crisis is the strange and unfamiliar outside world to us: the birds in the cage. We can either chose to stay in the cage which is the valley of death and await certain death and starvation, or step out of the cage taking courage in our hands to step into a different world.

In this type of situation, any person may go through four stages of thinking: -

a) Confusion – what to do?

b) Denial – no! Why no food and water? This can't happen!

c) Acceptance of the truth and new situation but not still sure – step out of the cage and peer around, meeting strange things, strange creatures, strange behaviors

d) Get fired up by a sense of purpose – find the park! Or the forest! Lead a new, challenging but FREE life on one's own will!

Some of us sadly may not cross the second stage, and some of us may think of stepping out of the cage out of compulsion, not knowing what to do. The purpose of this book was to help everyone of us step out of the cage and reach the fourth stage of thinking. When one gets fired up by a sense of purpose to find the park or the forest to lead a free and more fruitful life, counter intuitive thinking commences.

COUNTER INTUITION IS REACHING THE FOURTH STAGE OF THINKING.

It's thinking what you normally will not think. It's attempting to do what is deemed crazy and impossible. No one ever thought Croatia will be one of the finalists! There is a famous saying: - "be brave then mighty forces will come to your aid". The process of counter intuitive thinking commences when you first decide to be brave! This then is the starting point, the decision to find the park or forest – just not stepping out of the cage, but overcoming your fears to find the park of forest. Counter intuition occurs when mighty forces come to your aid – this is a common thread running through all the twelve stories we presented starting with abscess bursting, when Corbett was hunting the man eater to Croatia reaching the final to Captain Rajkumar taking off on a dark stormy night just on a hunch that there is someone out there who needs help! Counter intuition is not lighting a lamp in the dark! It's getting used to the dark and seeing in the dark! It is listening the sound of silence, it is dreaming big in empty pockets and having a deep faith that the dream will come true – this is the very heart of entrepreneurship and innovation.

Hence, we derive five key traits of counter intuitive thinking: -

1. Get fired up by a sense of purpose! You can find the park or the forest!

2. Its normal to be afraid – combat it, face it, listen your inner voice & control your impulses.

3. Believe in providence or miracle – it will happen! You can never step out of the cage, if you don't believe in miracles.

4. Combine the opposites – paradoxical thinking: This is the hardest part.

5. Battle your fear – then mighty forces will come to your aid.

The twelve knights of resilience are twelve different forms of counter intuitive thinking, demonstrating how it varies in different types of challenging situations. The list of twelve forms of counter intuitive thinking is not exhaustive, there can be many more. However, we are quite sure that these five principles will ring through in any challenging situation.

Innovating in the Valley of Death

Let us revisit the questions raised at the end of chapter 2: -

1. What business are we in?

2. What new competences can we build?

3. What was good and is no longer good?

4. What practices will become irrelevant very soon?

5. What unexpected events to expect?

6. Who are not our customers?

7. What are the key strategic risks that can hit us hard and cripple us?

8. How to build technology-human interfaces?

9. Where we need to take a more than calculated risk?

10. What is the bigger cause or purpose that will propel us through

the adversity?

These are the questions a manager or an entrepreneur must ask, in a valley of death situation such as the current one. Start by stating and discussing three beliefs with your team:

- *See light in darkness*

- *Listen the sounds in silence*

- *Forego the pleasures of life – often foregoing requires immense strength but paves way for something better and bigger!*

These three beliefs will help you find answers to the twelve questions. Then apply the five principles of counter intuitive thinking to find detailed answers. Last but not the least, to execute your strategy, when you have left the cage follow the framework suggested below:

1. Building collective resilience – coordinate internally and externally

2. Delivering more with less – collaborate extensively

3. Have faith when you are onto something big – co-evolve with the environment.

Thus, there are three principles of innovation in valley of death: - Coordination – Collaboration - Co-Evolution. These three principles will be dealt more extensively in the second book of the two-part series.

AFTERWORD

This book was then meant to take you out of the cage, giving you the courage, hope and bring you to the state of mind to find your park or forest! So that you can lead a meaningful life with freedom! The idea of twelve adventure stories was to take you into the larger arena of life, beyond your office into the thrill of facing a deadly adversary in a thick forest, reliving the thrill and excitement of a world cup football final, the tension of war with specter of death hanging over or going off on a roller-coaster ride with Captain Rajkumar!

Counter intuition is a powerful and difficult mode of thinking, not easily put to practice. These twelve stories amply demonstrated various types of counter intuitive thinking in different situations. However, they are not exhaustive and more variants may emerge out of more such thrilling stories. But we are quite sure that the five principles of counter intuitive thinking are universal and will stand out in any story of crisis management and triumph, be in war, sports, business or politics or in an individual's struggle for dignity in life.

Thank you for being with us! We hope you enjoyed reading this book and started your preparations to walk out of the cage to find your forest of freedom!